THE WEEPING GODS OF MANIPUR

The Crying Rains and the Blood Lilies

(A political Treatise)

Hijam Monarsingh Dallo Rihmo
Manipur

Manipuri Neo Communism- 10.5281/zenodo.14838006
Law and Order- 10.5281/zenodo.14838025
Manipur Needs to Affirm her Tribal Roots- 10.5281/zenodo.14840161
The Sciences of Co Option in other Nations and Manipur- 10.5281/zenodo.15105130
Manipuri Political Consolidation and Three State Theory- 10.5281/zenodo.15072522
Manipur Crisis Solution Proposal: Phased, Modular and Hybrid and other Models- 10.5281/zenodo.14945568
FMR Upgrade 2025- 10.5281/zenodo.14845612
1961 NRC Base Year Justification, Manipur- 10.5281/zenodo.15105670

The work is a collection of most plausible patterns from observation and it does not advocate nor oppose any political objective. It projects and predicts, if these 'patterns' develop un-hindered. Some of the work draws elements of governance from tribal and historical evidences. The samplings and extrapolation are based on specific count of datasets and it is possible the results may vary with the increase or decrease of data/information. The book unlike other papers may appear less rigorous and has few examples, as these ideas in my opinion are either new or never practiced earlier. While also acknowledging that it is possible to find similarities. The book aims to encourage discussion and hopes to find a place in schools and universities, where these ideas will be rigorously studied and given a proper definition that it lacks, in that it is for academic purpose, the hope is that these ideas can hope to form the foundation of more effective and better policies and laws that also respects local specificities. The book does not support secessionist ideas. The book tries to draw ideas comparatively from all forms of governance. In that, it believes in an evolving government, in short it uses them as foundations. The critique in the book is meant to provoke thought and not disregard and or discredit any organization or government. As it is, in a democracy the governance structure is often judged based on leadership, effective governance, perception and the stability and transparency of an 'Ideal' government.

"Only a person who has no love for his land
nor mother would avoid politics.

The first step in protecting your own, is
being political."

Political Treatise on Manipur

The book is the second series of 'The Weeping Gods of Manipur'. The first series, *'The Crescent Highlands and the Dark Rainbows'*, intends to make readers understand the nature and very essence of time that shaped the Manipur we know today. What brought Manipur to where it is now.

The second series, 'The Crying Rains and the Blood Lilies,' contains the following theories;

1. The Creation of Chandel (Theory from Oral Tradition)

2. Affirmative actions, reservation threshold of 40:60 theory. Manipur & Bangladesh.

3. The Manipuri Neo Communism
4. Manipuri Politics Parties and the consolidation into a Binary Spectrum

5. The Need for Manipur to affirm her tribal roots, Scheduled Tribe Hills and Scheduled Tribe Plains

6. The Three State Theory

7. The Sciences of Co-Option: In Manipur and other Nations

8. The Free Movement Regime and its Upgrade

9. Law and Order Visualization of Manipur

10. Manipur Crisis Solution Proposal: Phased, Modular and Hybrid and other Models

11. The National Register of Citizens

12. NRC: Why 1961 as base year for Manipur and not 1951.

When souls fly into the blue blue sky

When your souls,
They fly into the blue blue sky.
Weep as much as you can,
Weep as much as you can.
When your souls,
They fly into the blue blue sky.
Tell the Gods what they did to you,
Tell the Gods how they treated you.
When your souls,
They fly into the blue blue sky.
Weep as much as you can,
Weep as much as you can.
The people you leave behind,
Let them feel the tearful tearful rain,
Let them feel the tearful tearful rain.
Fly away now into the blue blue sky,
Fly away now into the blue blue sky,
Weep as much as you can.

(The book is pain, the book is anguish, the book is memory. Listen, hear what the book has to say when it still speaks.)

The Premise

I was told it makes no sense going back in history and trying to justify. And indeed, it makes no sense if its justification we are looking for.

Society and even religion evolve over time, it's like undoing all the things the society has learnt only to repeat. Ethnonationalism and its grip over Northeast India and especially Manipur, is undoubtedly very intense, a cursory search and or reading and the opposite is "Civic Nationalism". I don't excel in any discipline nor do I have an in-depth knowledge of anyone subject, my interest too, ever so fleeting and the environment I am in, ever so fragile. One statement and I would have to think over a hundred times over if it may have offended anyone one group, which I unfortunately do any which way. I watch TV discussions diligently and so often, I feel like I know the panelist in person now, like as if they live next to my house. It is a little disappointing how despite the many discussions we don't seem to be making any headway progress. Still stuck in the violence, there are lulls but what of it when it is only waiting for a chance to erupt. Every instance growing more and more gruesome. I make lengthy post on social media and in fact collated all of them in a book I will never publish. The language utterly crude and the sentences, they speak in an accusatory tone. It's almost like a diary anyway, but I did write hoping it touches some turning points and perhaps reflect the evolving socio-economic condition of the state over decades. I was growing in that 'space'. But it is at best and still remains an attempt. There are aspirations and sentiments which arguably cannot be dismissed. The current contest apart from the violence is the demand for the Schedule Tribe (ST) status by the Meiteis and the demand for a Separate Administration.

This arrangement can be made possible though. I see it is only to do with the examination and recruitment. So, the ST will have to be differentiated in my opinion. The ST for Meiteis (STM if you want to call it) be made applicable for the districts; Imphal East, West, Kakching, Bishnupur, Jiribam & Thoubal. If the districts are reorganized, a gazette notification in relation to the districts covered should suffice, I hope. I don't know how things work in the department, my logic is simply dividing the same examination, same question paper into two sections each with varying vacancies with respect to the districts itself. So, in effect, the Meiteis compete between the Meiteis only to address the fear of Meiteis taking over in the state recruitments. I don't think there is or this should be any problem beyond the state, as it will function normally like any other ST reservation. The ST for the remaining hill districts be applied as usual, their vacancies determined by the number of posts required in their districts. The postings however should not adhere to any such compartmentalization, that would only feed ethnonationalism. That in the long run is not good, perhaps temporarily the postings can follow the model owing to the violence but it should be avoided as best possible and done away with as soon as possible.

In relation to the land, If Moreh stops serving Manipur. The place will devolve – I am sure the people living there are already seeing signs of it. Imphal was its biggest market. To stimulate thrift in the economy you need population to create demand. So, regarding the land, I think the administration first need to introduce a "Permanent Land Settlement" system in the hills. So even if the tribal man sells the land, he gets compensated enough for it. This will help in the growth of the district headquarters itself and help create wealth and appreciate the prices of fixed or landed properties like rentals, land etc. The increased population will increase other secondary sectors including transport and services which will help the local economy grow. If he fears alienation, it is within him to grow richer and buy the same plot of land back from the person, he sold should the chance present it to his good fortune.

Regarding the separate administration, if the idea is for the growth of the districts itself, decentralization and a separate fund allocation from the central authority is actually desirable. Imphal has much chance of a faster growth if the hill districts start to demand more goods and services. That's actually how money circulates in the economy anyway. It does not infringe on the territorial integrity of the state of Manipur. I understand there are apprehensions, but Manipur joined the Indian Union as an entity. It will never break because breaking it would mean to break the Merger Agreement and it simply means giving back Manipur its independence.

It's understood, the emotions right now are still intense. This was only an argument which may be applied. But it may not be practical in the immediate months. It will perhaps take time and this writing I have made, now I'll have to sit and think over it a hundred times if it may have offended anyone. Like I said earlier, my language is most crude and I am no expert.

In this book, the area will focus more on the crimes leading to the violence of 3rd May, 2023. It was a crisis in the making for decades that exploded on that fateful day. Let me start here with the tribal societies and how it developed into district centers we now know. That will perhaps clear some confusion on the ownership battle taking place in Churachandpur. How between tribals with money they bought land (without ownership papers) and then fight among themselves that it belongs to their tribe. It is naturally so when ownership is tied to the community rather than the person. Manipur tribals in 2025 are essentially,

'Landless People'.

The Crimes of Manipur Government.

The Creation of Chandel

Like the Kangla when the earth, it birthed dry lands in the tiny valleys. The hillmen they say they lived on Keral-Lon. The site of this old village atop the hillock now lies abandoned. But they too silently tell stories like the ancient Phiral or the legendary Khullen and join the conversation of history. If the gods are kind and the signs are good, people would flock. Enough people to raise a monolith and call it home. Japhou started in the swamps with seven houses. The seven houses on a tiny Dryland like the Kanglas appeared in the Imphal valley. It's akin to the nature of life in the valleys of this rugged terrain, like it's a story of its childhood into adolescence. It's like the waters that were dammed, they finally broke and created rivers and drylands. First grasses then deers and then tigers. Then men and villages and then rice fields. How they finally tamed the lands and created settlements. And then larger settlement, a 'khul'. How Chandel came to being, then Hnatham, Lambung, Modi, Panchai and Cheengkhu. Then the Pantha (Upland), Damthra (Plateau), khulbol (foothills), the names of the places closely linked with the nature and topography of the place itself.

A very tribal way of naming them, names that describes its very nature. Time would shift and then the hillmen will become numerous, they will dance on harvest, create festivals, observe the moons and seasons and such. Create and 'live' tradition and culture. And between them choose for themselves hierarchy and develop societies and unions. It will in time, culminate in to tribal arts and tribal governance. They will go on to create events and host 'Alums'. Make for themselves a way of life that will forge their own tribal identity. An identity rooted in its past, present and future. And soon they will be identified as the tribals of the hills. The tribals of;

Chandel.

The story now three generations old. At the time of the storytelling, there will be the

Monsangs, the Zous, the Lamkangs, the
Chothe, the Aimol, the Murring, the Kukis,
the Moyon and Pakan-Anals.

Now if we relate this with Churachandpur,
before the town came into being it was
perhaps a cluster of villages. If the mix
ethnic makeup continued the fight between
the tribes wouldn't have taken place but
owing to the tribal administration in force. It
has to divide the territory, feudalism in
short. And therefore, we have the
Churachandpur in the news. Imphal to me
appears to be heading in the same direction.
Currently it affords tribal colonies and
Muslim colonies in between, but it only
enforces division in the capital itself only
waiting for a match just like Churachandpur.

Consecrating Tribal Settlements in Anaan-Pakan Tradition

The Customs

It is said that the Meiteis referred to the tribes as Anaan through their spoken law. To sort of likened it with their habit in maintaining the division of the clean' and the 'unclean.' Perhaps, it is also to do with their close association with the God, Wangparal or Wangbren. The God of disease and sickness, among many others.

The elder with the knowledge of worship, medicine, rituals and everything that embody the tradition of the tribes. By virtue of their knowledge, they are tasked with communing with the Gods and find for the tribes – settlements. Along with the chants, it will involve leaving three eggs in the place of choice, deemed appropriate to settle. After three suns and three moons, they shall break open the eggs. If they turn out rotten, it is forbidden and the tribe must therefore read the directions and continue the search. If the eggs do not rot however, it is the God's will and the tribe is blessed and they may settle with divine blessings. Prosperity and abundance.

Like the many tribes of Manipur, who reside around Kangla in colonies. The Anaan/Pakan tribe were settled in a colony close to a bridge (Around the present day Chingmeirong). The stories go on to tell how an epidemic broke out in the colony. And in relation to the customs, the tribe thus abandoned the area.

Where epidemics occur, it is customary for the tribe to abandon settlements. To stay is simply forbidden and is called 'Aadaang' in spoken rules of conduct. The colony now, is home to other tribes of Manipur. For the Anaan/Pakan, to not follow the laws passed down from generations would be an offence to the God, Wangparal. It appears he constantly guides the Anaan/Pakan Tribe. Shapeshifting, one time a serpent, the other time the image of a mortal.

And in his journey as a mortal, he will wed an Anaan/Pakan 'Shangnu'. The stones of the Khullen will stand as testimony of this Godly courtship that will blur the line between the Gods and mortals.

Tingnoupal, therefore as the name suggest, was so named after the God in anguish planted thorny bushes (Ting) to protect the Southern tribes and their settlements. In the story, the Anaan/Pakan are subjected to systematic killings and displacement from their villages and their fields by migrating tribes. And in her pain and hurt, Lord Wangparal' s Goddess cries out and implores Wangparal for divine intervention, the way her people died in the hands of the invading migrants. Wangparal was so moved he planted the thorny bushes round each settlement to please his Goddess.

The Goddess for whom he would also gift a golden bamboo canister to his mother-in-law. The mother who will immerse herself in the confluence of Chakpi and Imphal and from the belly of the river. She will pray and release from the eddying currents, the birth of wild animals and fragrant flowers effusing

and blessing the tainted red hills of Chandel.
The site of this eddying current will then
become the sacred grounds of Sugnu Lai
Harauba. An annual pilgrimage where the
God Wangparal himself will immerse in spirit
and soul with the land and living.

An act of God

The site of what was previously called the

'The Laiching'
(The Hills of the Gods).

**

And so, the traditions become inheritance
and they are passed down generations after
generations. The year is 1891. It is spring
and almost summer. The chief of a certain
village will refuse participation in the great
upheaval. He will refuse to render help in
the event taking place, by only breathing,
going quiet and becoming only a seer from
the hills. A fateful event that will become the
source of inspiration for arts, politics, history,
governance and;

'Clarity'.

The *'White Man'*, will therefore write and sign a declaration, a document of *innocence* of this one southern village. And to keep this declaration and preserve the memory in writing, he must keep it tight inside 'the' bamboo canister. They say, it was impossible, the tribe was too few and they had too little. Even if they so wished, they couldn't have help in any meaningful way. They appear to already help by silently observing, never telling. Becoming an instrument of a forgotten chronicle.

So, the bamboos, they intertwine with the fate and history and become tradition passed down from the time when man and mortal roamed these lands. A tradition passed down from tribe to tribe. A tradition like the many bamboo creations. A creation that will be shared across the 'Crescent Highlands', across ethnicities, across tribes and across communities. One that will become synonymous in the unfortunate subjugation and the people themselves becoming;

'The Beast of Burden'.

It will break the hearts of the many Gods
and the lands will tremble with sadness. The
rivers too will revolt against nature and flood
the plains in protest. But history will be
defiant and continue to speak the passing of
time. It is so fated and it now rest only with
the people, history will breathe and kindle in
them – a *desire*. It is unclear if the Gods have
grown weak, but it is the people who must
restore order in the Cosmos and;

'Please the Gods.'

Creating the Manipuri Power

The Kangla is an indigenous creation that shapes the power structure between the rolling plains of the valley and her rugged hills. The various tribes settle in the vicinity around Kangla and in turn, create a relationship with the broader hill districts surrounding the valley. Encompassing in folk lore what is understood as the *nine* hill ranges. Forming a fortress around the valley. The various colonies then become a cogwheel in the system that facilitates:

'The Manipuri Power'.

To destroy a tribal colony around Kangla is therefore in essence the abdication of control of the hill the colony it is related with. The arrangement by nature lays the foundation of Manipuri power, moving away from its past unsustainable – regular expeditions. The arrangement by nature lays the foundation of the;

'The Manipuri Identity'.

A multi-ethnic power center that negotiates and creates an un-spoken diplomacy, one that fosters interethnic cohesion and intertribal power mechanism. A system that has evolved and defines the state of Manipur. An original creation, it is what defines;

'The Manipuri statecraft'.

The colonies, they cement and function in other words as; deterrence. A crucial aspect of native governance. The primal source of authority.

Creating the Manipuri Cosmos

Nature willed and from it was born the chants of heaven and earth. The eternal will define the realms. Life will take shape and manifest as Primal Gods and Deities. In time the creation of the night and day in the era where the sky was governed by two Suns. An arrow that will shoot down one of the suns. It will create the duality that will eventually become the creation of the sacred waters of the *'Nungjeng'*. One that will become central in the cosmos, the abode of the god,

'Pakhangpa'.

The mortals in their divine imitation of the Gods will speak languages and chronicle their existence blending and weaving the creation of the 'State'. It will ritualize and from its tribal units of counting, distances in fists and arms, and years in sticks and chants. It will create an entity of

remembrance, one that will become central
in tracing its own existence. The almost
sacred; the primary and breathing book will
come into existence;

'The Cheitharol Kumpaba'.

The birth of dissent; therefore, the land will
birth the tongue of dissent and create
passages in the chronicles written in the ink
of desire and etched in the struggle of
cosmic order.

It will herald conscience of clarity and truth
in every living and give them the five key
elements;

Courage
Honor
Valor
Justice
Truth

– The penta-foundation of the return to
cosmic order. The realignment of the Gods,

the sky, the earth, and their *'will'* from the
four corners;

The Thangjing
The Wangbren
The Marjing
The Koubru

It is inevitable; thus, it is ordained. And the
chronicles, therefore, they continue to
breathe and give the people a 'voice';

'A Culture'

– Of profound indigenous divinity. The
continuity of the *Manipuri*.

Mankind and his Thoughts

Thinking is I feel a continuous conscious activity. The book here is one such endeavor that didn't exist in thought nor in any other parallel. Like the book, 'The Weeping Gods of Manipur,' this book is born out of the latest tragedy, a tragedy so vile, it is an abomination that has shaken the very foundation of Manipur. For the first time in the history of Manipur, there is a radical shift. It is self-inflicted, it is like a mother killing her own child. This book is a twin to the;

'The Weeping Gods of Manipur.'

The concept of Naga Nation and Kuki Nation is to be understood in the tribal way. They are essentially stateless and for them nation comprises of people and therefore it places more importance on the people than land. The land automatically is the territory they reside in. This is undeniably visible in the fight for Nagalim and Zalengam. But times have changed, we have modern day borders now. Homeland- be it Kuki or Meitei or Naga, lesser humans that they are assumed to be evident from the way they have been treated, their homeland is divided arbitrarily in to two. No one cared or bothered that the people will be divided. But unlike Bangladesh and what is now Pakistan, the people did not accept it or simply didn't understand the foreign modern concept of nations and borders. And then came all kinds of extraordinary border rules like Free Movement Regime (FMR). I do not know how valid is such instrument but at the world stage, it's going to be a class of experiment that is almost unheard of. To put it bluntly it is almost a cruel joke, presented to the world as a humane gesture. Historically it has become the reason for many movements that has resulted in many untold tragedies that are vilified and justified as fight against terror. It begs the question here, who is the intruder and who conducts terror.

Currently as I write this page, the government has decided to fence the border like any other country. But now the tribal bodies are protesting. In effect, all these 75 years they did not realize that their homeland was divided into two, this is true for the common tribal folk. The consciousness only came very late, they are like almost caught unaware. It is sadder they were made to feel it is nothing, by introducing concepts like FMR. That they can travel to either country without any problem. A very dishonest instrument. It served its purpose for a while, if the partition happened the way Pakistan and India were divided it is clear, India was going to have another partition horror in the East. The way I see it, it would have invited war from the South East Asian Nations. 75 years later, now it is only small parties of tribals protesting and no one really cares from the looks of it. The government does not even need to act on it. It is now, 'harmless'. If this was 75 years ago, it would have sparked a regional war. But now the 'divided' tribals are divided into the following divisions; The largest one being Chinram – Mizoram in India and Chin Hills in Burma. Naga Nation – Nagaland in India and half in the adjoining parts of Burma, just like Manipur and Kabaw Valley.

These are historical facts drawn from books that are freely available in the public domain. Anyone can verify these matters I have pointed out anyway. It is no research, but these facts provide a much better foundation for what I will try to attempt in my discussions the various theories that are deeply intertwined with the hills and valleys and the people of this region;

The Crescent Highlands.

Therefore;

'I write about Manipur, her pain, her tragedy, her anguish, her dreams and hopes. I talk with her hills and trees, her orchids, her grasses and flowers, I whisper with her wind and float with her clouds and hum together with her rain. In her rocks and stones, I etch memories and songs. In her valleys I whisper with her echoes. And in her forest, I dream together with Manipur. In her pain and sorrow, I bloom with her lilies in colors and

colors and in her misery and tragedy I imitate and weave the movements of the Gods.'

The book will attempt to elicit Manipur's nature, politics, social make up, her wants and her story. And in a broader sense, 'The Crescent Highlands.'

File photo from the internet

Affirmative actions, reservation threshold of 40:60 theory.

Manipur & Bangladesh.

The affirmative actions have serious drawbacks when it comes to social and community living. Manipur is already a 'burning' example. The threshold ratio is likely 40:60 given the Manipur experiment (40 being the beneficiaries).

Affirmative actions on the other hand risks exclusion to the other party. It is by nature, an extremely strong political polarization tool.

Bangladesh also broke around 40:60 ratio.

Other countries with *Racial/Ethnic Based* reservation policies that touched the 40% threshold and erupted in violence.

- Sri Lanka Civil War (1983- 2009) It possibly resulted in the formation of the LTTE as well or at least played a major role. Touching 40%.

- Malaysia: Bumiputera Violence 1969, averaging 45%.

- Rwanda Reservation: 1961, Ethnic based policies resulting in the Rwanda Genocide 1994. Averaging 40%. The anomaly in Rwanda is very similar to Manipur Quota Based Violence.

- India- Our very own Mandal Commission. India is already witness to Quota based violences in different parts of the country. Manipur being the latest episode. National Quota averaging 49%.

The Manipuri Neo Communism

Introduction

The world has learnt from Democracy, that it did not deliver what it promised in the French Revolution and hence Socialism and Unionist, they were born out of it. Then we had the Communist form of government. In the 21st Century, we already have shining examples of Communist success. The Communist world has evolved in thought and ideology and become 'Neo Communism'. In the context of Manipur, although the native state has not had the chance to develop its own form of government unhindered. It did give birth to its own form of ideology rooted in its traditional past that still reverberates. However, to adopt 'Communism' as is defined in classic ideas or textbooks will probably not work, but Manipur would benefit if it picks from the leading communist countries with a successful Communist form of governance in its more evolved form, what I will call the;

Neo Communism

The math is very simple, if there are ten pieces of land and ten persons in Manipur. The capitalist by way of Money power cannot buy nine pieces of land, and deprive the nine, only for the nine to fight over the remaining one piece of land. Manipur needs to embrace its problems and look for a radical change, and it starts with governance and leadership. Or perhaps, the people.

Manipur is a hill state in the Northeastern part of India bordering Burma. The 'Native State' is home to tribals of different ethnicities of which the Meitei tribe is the most dominant. The crescent highlands which are also called the 'Burma Arc' is home to these tribals who essentially fit the definition of the 'Stateless Nations'. The territory of these tribals is arbitrarily cut in two, where one half is part of India while the other half is in Burma. It is home to the longest running insurgency in the world. The tribal societies here are traditionally 'communist' in nature – they are traditionally almost an egalitarian society.

Most of the communist countries that are successful are governance systems that 'allowed' changes. The countries that exhibit this success if we look carefully are not 'communist' at all. I can say the same thing about democracy, no two democracies are alike and they don't function the same, nor are they 'democracies' as you define in a book. All of it have communist or socialist elements. In a true democracy, you'd have voted for every decision.

Similarly, the new communism or 'neo-communism' does not fit the definition of 'communism' as we know. It has elements of globalization, liberalism, free market and things that are against the very definition of 'collectivism' and more of capitalist nature. Essentially, what I'm trying to convey is- this

new system, 'nameless' but nicknamed 'neo
-communism', because I tend to believe in
centralized core for efficient decision and
task execution- this new system is;

*1. Where every system including democracy
is slowly conforming to;*
*2. Even communist systems are slowly
conforming to;*

I'd imagine a pendulum that sways one unit
less every time towards equilibrium. I only
mean progress in systems cannot be from
democracy alone, it can be from a 'new'
communist and it may have certain
advantage over democracy- which i feel has
too many problems, there's always the
chance of conflict (real or thought),
concentration of wealth, power to the few,
believes in capitalism and keeps the binary
alive; king & slaves; lords & serfs; employer
& employee. The systems in the real world
all tend to tilt toward; equilibrium. Here, I
shall define it as 'political equilibrium'.

I advocate neo-communism, because I see
the tribal and Manipuri society- they
essentially exhibit communist systems, we

are by tradition communist. Democracy is disorder and chaos in its truest sense. Our society works on 'order', its deeply rooted in the family that no government system can change it.

It is its very true nature of the tribal and also the Manipuri society.

(This is perhaps true of any of the tribal states in the Northeastern part of India.)

In the introduction of this article. China as an example was only meant to make the point that 'Communism' as we know is not valid anymore. That we ought to see and recognize what is China doing differently. I think the makers of the Indian Constitution had very little regard for the different ethnicities in the Northeast, tribes and people and the 'native' form of governance. They instead created Article 371, special and temporary provisions. It appears the government was reluctant in applying the democratic ideals or force the democratic institutions in these areas and instead allowed the proliferation of a hybrid form of governance that is unique. The efficiency and reliability are however a matter of study. This brings us to the question if the Indian democracy is even a democracy or is it a majoritarian oppression in relation to its Northeastern states. It sends very little number of ministers to the parliament. There is however affirmative actions but the efficacy is again subjudice.

The success of 'democracy' elsewhere, share not just one, but many commonalities; shared history, almost all of them are racially white, connected and overlapping borders, similar food and culture and many things- why democracy for them works, perhaps. I'm drawing the assumption from the fact that religion also somehow makes implementation of policies very easy.

On the contrary, when we talk about centralized central authority, we seem to put a blanket policy on all decision making. I don't mean it that way, there are certain decisions that needs to follow the centralized model for faster and efficient execution. I however acknowledge that there are others that may need deliberation and consensus. If I may here make the distinction between; political and economic perhaps it will bring more clarity in the urgency of matters. Let's take the military for example, we would want a centralized core, and regarding people affecting policies we would want a more democratic framework. We may call it liberal democracy, if you see from a democratic perspective. But if you look from an erstwhile communist, it would be a liberal-communist, or the neo-communism.

I simply cannot agree for public participation in every field, perhaps it should be limited to only things that affects the people. It should not be every instance like 'liberal democracy' would advocate. I feel government systems should develop processes and policies that will determine 'a way of doing things' and 'not keep voting every time and restarting the system. When the need arises, legislate and effect changes if the established process is not efficient or does not serve its purpose. If you'll agree, then the creation of new and accepted processes you see tend to identify themselves to be more of a 'collectivism', essentially how a communist system works;

'Order'.

And all this should be read within the context of the 'tribals' and of Manipur. Otherwise, there is simply no reason why I should choose between two systems. It's because of our tradition, the 'Manipur' context.

All systems tend to conform to 'order', democracy by nature is slow, communism by nature is fast. There is no arguing on this. Why it 'advocates', In the original post, the mention of picking from where the systems have attained the level of progress that merits discussion. It is only the nature of development.

These democratic nations, or the democracy functions well in a homogenous unit, or where the majority statistically has an overwhelming majority- why the notion of majoritarian oppression is commonplace in public discourse in democratic nations with a plural society. Why the concept of immigrants and demography is a major concern. Democracy appears to facilitate these ills. Where there are too many contesting parties, it is essentially 'chaos'. And nations to the east is home to varying degrees of ethnicities and groups with some of them exhibiting a 'Native' form of governance like example;

'Manipur'

Or the belt of stateless nations. Manipur alone is home to thirty-three tribes. Democracy was forced on it, but every Manipuri knows the state is nowhere close to democracy. The tribals themselves have formed themselves into blocs and there is now the contest of three political blocs, the Nagas, the Kukis and the Meiteis.

Coming to the other East and South East Asian nations. The Soviet and Mao's regime for that matter. They are exactly the reason why 'neo-communism' is more valid than the traditional counterpart. That the erstwhile communist or socialist has already evolved from its past mistake and if we do a bit of a study without prejudice, they are

more valid now to the modern world. They
have simply 'evolved'. In a large system,
democracy would mean not just slow but
almost a halt, a deadlock, indecisiveness. For
example, key projects in a democracy may
face hurdles delaying and escalating costs.
while on the whole undermining the nation's
progress. I think even after 'christening'
them as National projects even, they still
underwent massive setbacks.

For the Indian Democracy, the Singapore
model might inspire this 'evolving' system of
governance under a different name. The
broad nature of the Singapore model is
characterized by tight restrictions on political
rights ensuring stability but a more than
usual freer market economy, with one of the
lowest tax regimes. This in turn attracts
foreign investments and creates 'service-
oriented' economic model with high returns
and salary dramatically improving the quality
of life making the tight political control
almost compensated.

Conclusion: The hybrid democracy, appears to want to include certain communist elements, while the neo - communism appear to want to include certain democratic elements. Almost like a pendulum moving towards equilibrium.

'A political equilibrium'.

Manipuri Politics
Parties and the consolidation into a binary Spectrum

The understanding of Political Organizations in India has been, a 'Multi Party'. The true nature however is the factionalism within, which owes its nature to the foundation of its formation, a multi ethnic society. The phrase, 'Multi Party', is thus an invented accepted definition. In effect, these parties either fall in the;

Left or Right

spectrum. Therefore, the idea of a multi-party system is but a 'myth'. They are in fact varying degrees of political parties that fall in either of the binary. The question of ethnicity, religion, society, identity too fall in between the binary in varying degrees. With this knowledge, it is clear that such parties or factionalism appear or occur due to the absence of an able 'Leadership'. The notion of leadership in this context, is abused to the extent that a failed person pushed to the helm but unable to lead any which way by way of position is called a "Leader", by virtue of his position. It becomes a definition of convenience. The social identity of the leader in question here — whether religious, ethnic or even class in turn serves in some cases, the groundwork for exclusivist narrative and the creation of a mental construct that borders supremacist ideologies. In the context of Manipur, this can be studied and for example can be attributed to all past "failed" leaders of Manipur. They have faced or had ample opportunity to lead, yet they couldn't. And in the run up for the next election, they come forward without any regard for their lack of leadership. The notion of the ethnicity of the leader to be, is also engineered to create a sense of justification to put in the position of leadership the choice of person. In relation to the topic, the formation of governments in Manipur appears to have evolved and experimented various forms;

- Centrally enabled state parties
- Coalition governments
- National parties

Of the three, National parties by nature seemed the most stable. But it failed in 2023. The nature of Manipuri grassroots political set up, now becoming increasingly divided into three noticeable variables only indicates it is headed for more "instability". By nature, you'd need an over-arching authority. Which means, Manipur theoretically has two options with a variable X;

- Accept increased external control for stability.
- Refuse external control and risk instability.
- *Variable X*

This however may not mean anything, where the 'variable' of an 'able' leadership is present. One that can cut across ethnicity and present a radical shift from the system that has long been the process of governance in Manipur. Historically, Manipur has seen no leader. Case by case study indicate the leaders per se have all exhibited the notion of a;

'Failed leadership'.

In the case of *variable X*, Manipur may find her own solution. In it, we are leaving the option open to changes that we may not be able to anticipate, a divergent variable. It could be systemic change, a radical shift in policy and or structural changes in administration, power shift (assuming it is fluid) or simply a 'leader.' This brings us to the next theory that takes into account the changing political reality

The History of the left and right of politics.

French Revolution (1789-1799), marked the start of the decline of monarchies. Summarily it is the seating arrangement of the French National Assembly. Those who were more inclined to tradition and supported the monarch sat on the right and those that can be termed revolutionaries, reformists etc. sat on the left. This system may not hold true any longer, but the idea of left- or right-wing politics is gaining traction. It is perhaps prudent for political parties to identify themselves for the purpose of 'Unification' and lesser chaos. It gives them an orientation. In India the bicameral nature of the assembly divided into Upper and Lower house by design is supposed to limit excesses, in other words;

"A second chamber is an indispensable security for freedom... it moderates the despotism of a single assembly." – John Stuart Mill.

But in recent politics in India, this has become synonymous with majoritarian control. Also, by the end of reading this paragraph, it becomes quite evident despotism can take place at every parallel and at every stage of governance.

The Need for Manipur to affirm her tribal roots, Scheduled Tribe Hills and Scheduled Tribe Plains

If the passages of the many books that details the account of the authors. One will find curious mention of the Meitei King and his connection to his tribal roots. If Sikhism is

the bridge between Hindu and Islam. Then
Manipuri, it would seem, is a bridge
between the dominant cultures, the Indian
and the Asian. An amalgamation of so many
influences that shapes the mesmerizing
culture we know today. Tribal by looks,
Hindu by religion, Asian by culture, Hill-men
by spirit – it seems as though it is a new
born civilization, the one we so fondly call –
The Meitei.

In the Meitei, there is the Shan element, the
Burmese, the Hindu influence, the Mosul
and predominantly the 'Tribals.' It is in fact,
the tapestry of the people that actually
makes the capital – Imphal.

The Meiteis, it would appear (the
amalgamation, & different from Khuman,
Moirang or Luwang) are a product of the
Shans, and many other 'people' who came
across the valley. Possibly settling and
establishing the kingdom of Manipur with its
center at Modern day Imphal. The Meiteis
will amalgamate all other chiefdoms in the
valley and bring about a uniform language
and culture, each clan perhaps contributing
an element in the tradition we know today.

The 'Manipur Valley; unlike the hills is an open space in the midst of the hills and if history is anything, anytime the valley was in danger or under attack, the population would seek shelter in the hills. This happened even in the Anglo – Manipuri war, and also during the *Seven Years* devastation where in the valley of Manipur underwent massive 'de-population'. Many of its inhabitants fleeing westward as far as Sylhet. Just like how the current crisis in Manipur is also driving away hordes of its affluent population. Manipur appears to be experiencing this symptom from time to time. The crisis now however, resulting in massive economic repercussions – the negation of wealth.

The capital in certain years, was recorded to be 'Keke Moirang'. This fact, is also supported by how the 'Revivalist' centers in Imphal now, confirms that there was many 'Kanglas' in the past. Indicating the capital or chiefdoms of each principality. This also tells us the valley of Manipur was a marshy swamp grassland earlier with parts of the higher ground appearing as habitable dry land (The Kanglas).

The Meitei identity is so unique due to the intermingling of different races, they have inadvertently become a new 'breed' of highland people. The younger generations without affinity to its past heritage. Tribal but unable to come to terms with it. Afterall, the valley is the heart and therein, everyone converges and mingles. Resulting in assimilation in her more modern civilized nature. From chaos, conquest and amalgamation to cultural domination and assimilation, and with it the birth of new surnames within the Meitei Society, losing its old self and reborn into the Meitei fold.

The Meitei itself appears a mixed race of which the tribals in the hills are perhaps the most that contributed to the mix (Inter community marriages and inter-tribal marriages). While the occasional dominance of other advanced cultures resulted in the paradigm shift – religion, architecture, rituals, food – all this, while maintaining a bit of her former self. In the making of the Meitei Culture. The story of Kangla itself is of one, wherein, the King moved from this traditional residence of a 'Naga House' into the more Shan-like residence. Its inhabitants later imitating the courtyard-architecture, just like the Shans. From the Ahoms; from wooden houses to the 'wattle and doab.' The similarities all too telling.

Manipur as a Hill state politically should have all its inhabitants designated as Tribals, it is only correct to curb the hardening divide between her own people. There is the apprehension from her less-privileged people who live in the hills. It is only natural to feel so. But laws are made my man and in the course of time and evaluation of what is good and what is wrong are born ethos and values that shape the society.

Factoring in political realities that are positioned to shape the political landscape of Manipur, perhaps the arrangement can be made if all Manipuris are recognized as tribals that they are, but to address the competition that may arise, there is a need to differentiate the population – Scheduled Tribe (Hills) and Scheduled Tribe (Plain).

Note: Assam SC & ST (Reservation in vacancies and posts in services) Act, 1978 as amended in 2012.

 In the act above Assam state has made differentiation in the Tribal groups. It affords inclusive development but also avoiding the competition within the same group as the ST (Plain) would also mean it will have a defined territorial limit, the reservation however, based on their population percentage. It is ideal and can be replicated in the state of Manipur. Perhaps this needs more deliberation from the stakeholders together. To discuss and understand each other's problems and apprehensions.

Manipur unlike the other states have much work to do including introducing a *"Permanent Land settlement system"* for her tribals and creation of wealth in the hills. A prosperous hill district is after all a prosperous valley. The growth and development of the hill and valley being interdependent.

The Three State Theory

This abstract application *takes* key factors for the purpose of calculation. In real world these factors that serves as anchors for calculation may not hold true although the assumptions are largely correct in my opinion. With that knowledge in mind, if we treat Meitei Kuki and Naga as 'Set Objects' mathematically, then by that set theory;

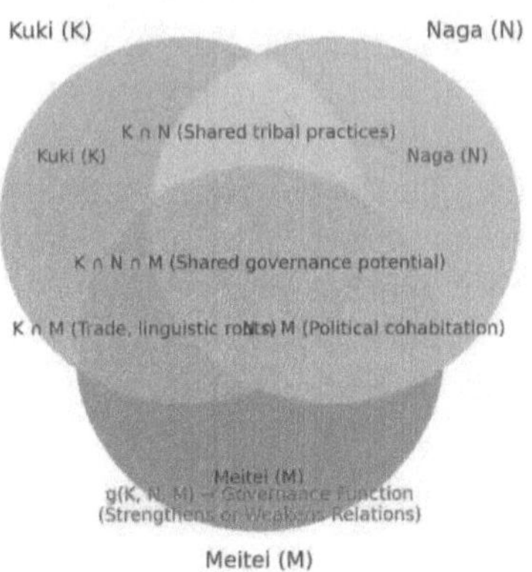

Set Representation of Kuki, Naga, and Meitei with Governance Function (g)

The diagram for the set theory is AI – Generated image. Explanation of the diagram; In the set example above we assume three separate entities with;

Governance function (g);
K – Kuki
N – Naga
M – Meitei

Now the Set Intersections
- K n N- shared tribal practices
- K n M- Trade and linguistic roots between Kuki and Meitei.
- N n M- Political cohabitation between Naga and Meitei.

Therefore (K n N n M) Shared governance potential among Kuki, Naga, and Meitei.
Governance Function g (K,N,M)

- The function g(K,N,M) represents governance policies, laws, and administrative decisions that either strengthen or weaken intercommunity relations.
- This function is crucial because it determines how well Kuki, Naga, and Meitei coexist politically and economically.

Calculations for Set Operations;

1. Union (U)

- KuNuM = The total set of all three communities, including

all individual and shared elements.

2. Intersection (n)

- K n N Number of shared elements (tribal practices).
- K n M Number of shared elements (trade, linguistic roots).
- N n M Number of shared elements (political cohabitation).
- K n N n M Number of shared elements in all three groups (governance potential).

3. Complement (')

- K' = All elements not in Kuki but possibly in Naga or Meitei.
- N' = All elements not in Naga but possibly in Kuki or Meitei.
- M'= All elements not in Meitei but possibly in Kuki or Naga.

(Although the ideas of seeing humans in set objects is original. The calculations are made on assumed facts and uses AI to create the conditions and possible favorable outcomes. The above example aims to serve as a possible framework model.)

Therefore, with the examples above, we can conclude that the governance potential lies in the "Shared elements". The political construct in reality is based on ethnicity, religion or purity in contemporary Manipur. The definition of shared elements must move away from these traditional definitions into more progressive and forward approaches like, pop culture, cinemas, music, sports, education, sciences, businesses etc. Under each of this head, the world has more to offer Manipur in each vertical, which also has the potential to amplify business opportunities and thereby wealth.

Now, with the framework calculation above, assuming it is mathematically correct. The identification of the political reality is real and is backed with mathematical abstracts that are by nature of its own definition accurate and precise. In the context of power-balance, the current structure has two Lok Sabha Member of Parliaments; the Inner and Outer Member of Parliament (MP). Taking into consideration the formation of a political power in the southern districts. It becomes imperative to have a third MP to balance the equation. The argument is simple, it's un-democratic to have the third group, 'under-represented'.

Despite the lack of population, this becomes a strong case for a democratic country that 'boast' the largest democracy. The country should set an example and turn the 'International Embarrassment' as is defined frequently in news and media, into a show of a strong functioning example of Indian Politics.

This also complements, the ST (Plains) and ST(Hills) proposal where the idea of Manipur affirming her roots is contested. While it awards the benefits desired, social, government and also territorial, it also effectively separates 'Administrative topology' from 'Social topology'. The Administration being, a stronger ADC and a territorial council for the valley reporting to the head of the state the Chief Minister. In relation to land rights, there are various proposals and options and suggestions like controlled spaces like SEZ concepts that can be explored. In addition, the government also has the option to introduce a permanent "Hill Land Settlement System". This would mean discussions between all stakeholders. The access to the capital however cannot be under the dominant control of one ethnicity alone. so Imphal must function like;

Shillong.

Like a state capital. And not an ethnic bastion. Perhaps in line with recent developments. Transform the Imphal boundary into a capital territory. Or create a new capital, culturally neutral and letting Imphal develop organically rather than impose an administrative responsibility, given its years of history.

Land Laws – It is perhaps prudent to repeal the MLR & LR Act for a new Land Law for the entire state. Maybe the state of Manipur needs to *synthesize* a new land law that recognizes the political reality and the aspirations of all the communities.

Reasons for a new land law;

- Imposition of MLR&LR is opposed by the hill districts.
- MLR&LR itself is a poorly framed policy (The MLR&LR Act, is fraught with issues).
- Repealing is a much better option than fixing MLR&LR.
- Creating a new land law in consultation and consensus with all stakeholders Kuki, Naga and Meitei is the correct way forward.

Land law is a state subject and sooner the assembly is functional this perhaps will be the first step towards resolution finding. A new land law avoids the problems and apprehension associated with the MLR&LR Act which is anyway opposed by the hills and is also not without problems itself.

At this point, we must also factor in the recent political development in the southern districts of Manipur where Civil Societies have floated a proposal to introduce a permanent land settlement system. The question of whether the organization can really make an impact is uncertain however for the purpose of record, the translation as accurate as possible;

Translation;

WORLD KUKI-ZO INTELLECTUAL COUNCIL (WKZIC) (Former Kuki-Zo Intellectual Forum). HEADQUARTERS: SONGPI-LAMKA, INDIA - 795128 (Conglomerate of Chin-Kuki-Mizo-Zomi-Hmar-Mara-Ralte-Khumi Blood Ethnic). Email: wkzic822@gmail.com.Ref.No.179/WKZIC-GHQ/(PR)/2023-25. Date: 23rd March 2025

To,
The President/Secretary,
Kuki Chiefs Association Manipur (KCAM),

Subject: Proposal for a Referendum on the "KCA Land Holding Modifications Act 2025" by the Kuki Chiefs Association Manipur (KCAM) Assembly.

Respected Sir,
First and foremost, the Kuki-Zo people and the WKZIC extend our greetings. We are aware that the esteemed village chiefs and senior leaders of KCAM are convening an assembly on the 27th of March 2025 at Songpitol, Tuibuong, to discuss critical matters concerning our land and community. The WKZIC deeply appreciates this initiative and wishes to highlight the importance of this assembly for the welfare and unity of our people. In light of the current challenges faced by our community, it is imperative that the voices of the people ("MIPI AWSO") are heard and considered in the agenda.

*1. *Land Holding:* The WKZIC Mission Team visited the "TWICHIN-PHAIMOL GROUPING CENTRE" on the 5th and 6th of March 2025 and engaged with the people, the Kuki Inpi (KIBB), and SAHILCA. We urge the village chiefs/KCAM to deliberate carefully on the systematic and fair* *redistribution of land, ensuring the welfare of the community under the guidance of the esteemed chiefs.*

*2. *Referendum:* For over a century (105 years), the Kuki people have endured immense suffering, with our lands encroached upon by others. From 1956 to 2023, we have lost approximately 606 square miles of land. In this context, the need for a "Deidan Vetllnahna" (REFERENDUM) to reclaim our ancestral lands, as initiated during the Kukiland movement of 1946-47, is more pressing than ever. This referendum must be conducted under the authority and wisdom of the village chiefs.*

i) British Mombi (Lonpi) Area 1907
ii) British Chassad Area 1907
iii) British Jampi Area 1907
iv) British Songpi Sub-Division 1919

- Chandel KCA & Tengnoupal KCA
- Ukhrul KCA, Kamjong KCA & Saikul KCA
- Kangpokpi SAHILCA, Jiri-Noney-Tamenglong KCA
- Churachandpur KCA & Zomi Chiefs Association (ZCA)

3. Multiple Referendum: Churachandpur/Songpi is a diverse region, comprising:
a) Haokip Reserved,
b) Dampi-Haopi (Part of British Mombi Area 1907),
c) Manliur Region,
d) Guitekaul,
e) Singson Region & Hmar Biel (Part of British Jampi Area 1907),
f) Thangsing Area,
g) Vatiphei Area,
h) Gangie Area, etc.

Each of these areas should be addressed according to the customs and traditions of the respective tribes.

(T. SAMUEL ZOU) General Secretary
(L. TUNTA NGAIHTE) Vice-President, Cust & Cult.
(DR. TS HAOKIP) President

In conclusion, the need for Manipur to recognize all its citizens are tribals is already laid out in the first section. This is followed by the Three State Theory, where all three different components report to the head of the state. In relation to the land reforms, the tribal societies have themselves taken up the matter in connection with their chiefs. This political development is bound to alter the political reality of Manipur – radically.

The Sciences of Co-Option: In Manipur and other Nations

It is in our history too. Whenever external agencies get the chance to interfere, they co-opt and turn events to their advantage.

Bangladesh, the protest for a limit of reservation that crossed well over 50% threshold (assumed but theoretically it holds), violence broke out. But the suppressed antigovernment forces co-opted and the protest resulted in the ouster of the premiere, Sheikh Hasina. If we study the power dynamics, it was impossible to topple her regime, but it fell apart. Historically, Manipur too gave external agencies the opportunity to co-opt in its internal matters and it led to the Seven Years Devastation, personally I don't think Manipur has never recovered from it. It became a protectorate and never a sovereign after.

Dozens of royalists injured in clashes with police fuelled by political instability and economic discontent

Nepalese police firing teargas to disperse pro-monarchy demonstrators in Kathmandu. Photograph: Prakash Mathema/AFP/Getty Images

Now in Nepal, the presence of pro-monarchy elements has given the opportunity to agencies that have co-opted to mount pressure and create instability.

What does this mean for Manipur. Contemporary Manipur has created not just one but many faults in its relations with her people and other agencies. It has by now seeded many reasons for a series of instability that if co-opted can rock the edifice of its very existence. Be it social, cultural, economic or political- Manipur has managed to create a rift in every sphere. If co-option takes places, it will continue to be unstable like a series of unending cycles.

"Her Hallmark."

It is for the people to understand, co-option may not be visible but they are undeniably present in every political event. They appear, to be born out of every such event in a state.

To me- "If Manipur cannot fix herself, she has no right to complain about exploitation. It is self-inflicted."

About the article, if indeed India's agency has co-opted then, India has perhaps realized that democracy is always prone to external manipulation. Although the veracious claim is unfounded but theoretically yes. This also explains why Pro-Monarchist are gaining widespread popularity. The initiation of Chinese influence with the BRI in the region was in the news a few months ago. This was preceded by the advertisement of Tibet's transformation- manipulation of sentiments. And it appears to have worked. So, for India, will India embrace a more centralized democracy to avoid the fate of other weak democracies then? Is Monarchy truly the only way to stop Chinese aggression, what about borderlands like Manipur. Will India still call "Neo Communism" seditious, or see reason in the political theory. One that is deeply aligned with the tradition of Manipur itself. A perfect framework for Manipur's "Self-Governance" model. Given the 'Three State Theory, and the creation of two ADCs and one Territorial Council. The "Manipuri Neo Communism" paper becomes viable.

The Truth is democracy is like a container, it can also contain "Traditional" and or "Manipuri Neo Communist" elements- a blend of democracy and communism;

"An Equilibrium".

A perfect instrument that will shield Manipur from external manipulation. India cannot afford an unstable Northeast. It also risks exposing herself to external agencies that way, as I have attempted to explain in- "The Sciences of Co-Option." It is in the very nature of conflicts or events, over time;

"They Evolve."

Then, is "Democracy", really immune to external influences. The way I see it, economic domination is influencing policy decisions in all other lesser democracies.

Is this beyond neo-colonialism and modern-day colonialism where true power is wielded through other means rather than brute force —

"Compulsion."

The Free Movement Regime

The Free movement regime or FMR is a policy that allows people on either side of the Indo-Myanmar border to move within each territory without any document. Recently, owing to the Manipur violence the scrapping of the FMR became imminent and a new FMR policy was effected;

1. Introduction of Border Passes : The new system means that the entry will be regulated through 43 border crossing points where Assam Rifles (AR) personnel will issue "border passes".

2. Single Entry: The pass will permit only one person for a period of 7 seven days at a time with the permit to move up to 10 kilometers from the Indo-Myanmar border.

3. Return: The passes have to be returned to the same crossing point where the pass was issued.

The holders of the border pass will be permitted to enter the border 10km area for the following purposes; visits, tourism, medical, business, sports, official duty, meetings, cultural exchange programs and such. It still tries to respect the cultural ties and such but ill not delve into it and leave the links at the end of the page for further reading if it interests.

In short, the distance was reduced from 16 to 10 kms and anyone crossing the border had to simply show some sort of identification. It does not prohibit or stop the movement the undocumented border crossing simply was documented. The media house's choice of word like 'scrap' may have played a role, also the construction of the border fence may have simply created the confusion.

All these, came very late and failed to served any purpose in relation to the violence. The authorities able to effect any change except antagonising communities. The Manipur Violence had already sort of stemmed by the time the changes were brought about. The benefits of these changes however still remain to be realised. At the time of writing this article, the Union has completed 30 kilometres of fencing at a cost of 31,000 crores with the completion estimated to be in within 10 years time.

The proposed upgrade of the FMR

 Autonomy: Considering 10 km each from either side or maybe 16 kms from the earlier FMR. Both India and Burmese government to recognise and establish an autonomous zone to be created from both country.

Nature: This zone will be completely autonomous and will try to address the insurgency, self determination and the many ethnic movements. The proposal is only an attempt to sort formulate a working autonomous body that will adress the socio-cultural and economic challenges of the region in a limited area. The region under the current FMR. If autonomy is not an option we have the choice of a special administrative region.

Broad Definition: A 'Shared Regime' where people from both India and Burma can settle, move and conduct freely within the region that will come under the autonomous body so constituted. The autonomous body will be developed as a joint, Indo-Burma institute that will function like a governing body for the FMR region. This will be a new body that will address both Indo-Burmese Interest (Joint Institution).

Conditions

- Security: The arrangement will attempt to address Burma's Ethnic Movement issues and India's Insurgency Movement.

- Emphasis: The arrangement perhaps should focus more on economic autonomy.
- The Centre may devise centrally controlled military and organization (in line with the Manipur Merger).

The paper attempts to only proposes a limited experiment in the FMR region only. It is a theory. The institute may perhaps function as a tripartite body centrally controlled, self-administered (autonomous) and in joint operation with Burma. This in line with the essence of 371c.]

Many of the demands earlier if I remember
it correctly from the local dailies, there was
proposals for a SAR (Special Administrative
Region), while a de facto Hongkong model is
not suited owing to the presence of other
contesting organizations. Perhaps the center
can, on the economic front allow the
following key provisions that shall benefit all
parties, for example;

- Zero or Near zero tariffs on imports
  and exports, this in line with the Act
  East Policy. The government may
  focus more on scale and the growth
  of other allied businesses.

- Minimal Trade Barriers and low
  taxation perhaps. It will be beneficial
  for the border states if India develops
  a bilateral agreement with Burma as
  members of ASEAN. The government
  may frame policies as required
  whether, direct engagement or
  through ASEAN or a hybrid, free
  dictation.

All these mentions are actually broad
working frameworks in the ASEAN, the

Regional Comprehensive Economic Programme (RCEP). For India, none of this would work without a stable border and this is where the Shared Regime comes into picture. We've tried the FMR, the way it is, It has largely failed and even become a threat to national security. We may now need to upgrade and for effective administration, perhaps a local autonomous administration. The region is already under the ADC (Autonomous District Council) anyway and also the FMR is an agreed bilateral arrangement with Burma. They are already in place. It only needs an upgrade. And if India wants to maintain effective control it can still continue to create Centre-State Autonomous Bodies.

Law and Order Visualization

A Preliminary Law and Order Report.

Report: The dots below indicate the incidences of violence and protest in Manipur taking 2017 as the base year.

Pre 2017, the incidences were localized and highly volatile with Imphal recording as much as 120 instances. The average was 41.5 instances on average. The number of major sites affected was a tally of 10. Churachandpur was the most disturbed hill district with 85 counts.

Top: Pre 2017 with 415 instances. | Bottom: Post 2017 with 204 instances.

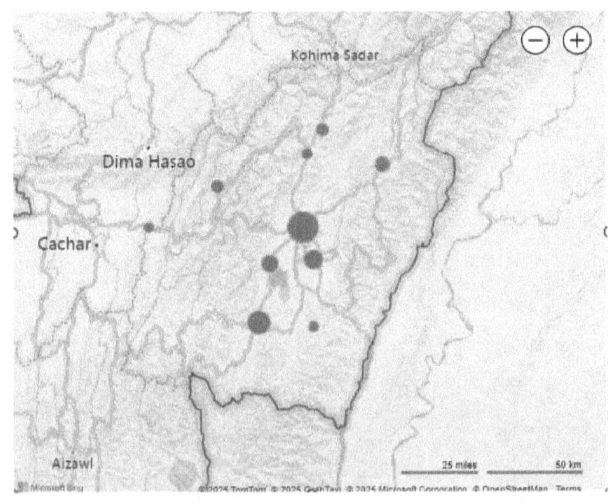

Kohima Sadar
Dima Hasao
Cachar
Aizawl
25 miles
50 km

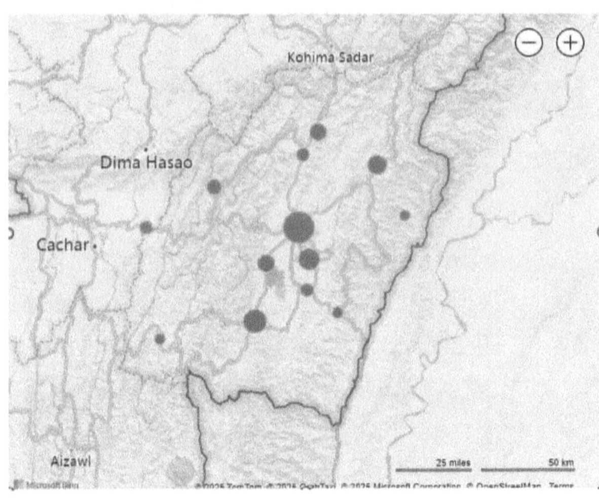

Kohima Sadar
Dima Hasao
Cachar
Aizawl
25 miles
50 km

The tally is over a period of 15 years. The average instance per year is 27.67 count.

Post 2017, the incidences were widespread and the entire state was under frequent law and order problem. Imphal recorded the highest number of instances at 45 counts. The average was 14.5 instances on average. The number of major sites affected was a tally of 14. Churachandpur was the most disturbed hill district with 30 counts.

The tally is over a period of 9 years. The average instance per year is 22.67 counts.

Law and Order in the hills

- Pre 2017, excluding Imphal, the district headquarters alone contributed an average record of a whopping 32.7 instances on average. Indicating a volatile law and order situation in the hill districts under the regime.
- Post 2017, excluding Imphal, the district headquarters alone contributed 12.23 instances on average. Indicating much improved

law and order situation in the hill
districts under the regime.

Inference: Government must ensure law and order in the state capital, deterioration at Imphal puts a compound effect on all districts. Sensitization of instability and its effects economic and social and awareness at various levels, institutions, CSOs and instilling democratic forms of protest. Or better, advise organizations to send in letters with their prayers or demands.

- The lower count of instances posts 2017 indicates an improving law and order situation that worsened since 3rd May, 2023.

Post 2017, the law-and-order situation in the hills greatly improved. In both the regimes Churachandpur district is most disturbed. Government may make efforts to find the causes of disturbances in Churachandpur and improve the L&O.

Government may create inter-district road connectivity to improve infrastructure and development. This will have a remedial impact on business and services and reduce inter tribe/community conflict. While improving economic viability.

- The average instances of L&O problems pre 2017 at 27.67 and post 2017 at 22.67 may indicate, citizens are experiencing almost the same problems under both the regime.
- In both pre and post 2017, there has been very little 'new' development initiative, most were upgradation work or centrally sponsored schemes. Efficacy is not measurable.

A more detailed report based on 20000 samples is included in the later chapters.

Manipur Crisis Solution Proposal: Phased, Modular and Hybrid and other Models

In continuation with the earlier findings. Below we have a more detailed summary attempt at presenting a possible framework for the crisis resolution. In it, I have taken the help of the law-and-order situation samples, the state's budget; to have a small understanding of the capacity and problems. The information is from government publications. Some of the information have been grouped together with similar sets to make it easier to comprehend. The crisis framework envisages a three-step model, that loosely follows a dependency sequence spread over a period of 15 years.

The Nature of the society

Manipur is a hilly state in the Northeastern part of India bordering Burma. The 'Native State' is home to tribals of different ethnicities of which the Meitei tribe is the most dominant. The crescent highlands which are also called the 'Burma Arc' is home to these tribals who essentially fit the definition of the 'Stateless Nations'. The territory of these tribals is arbitrarily cut in two, where one half is part of India while the other half is in Burma. It is also home to the longest running insurgencies in the world. The tribal societies here are traditionally 'communist' in nature – they are traditionally almost an egalitarian society. The spirit of collectivism is by default a part of it.

Problems

Law and Order: Summarily under different terms, the law and order worsened from localized and highly volatile situation to a more widespread and frequent one. This was based on a limited random sampling of 619 reports. Expanding the samples to

21530, we get key information that points to one crucial factor – 'inadequate policing.' The problem is more pronounced in the hills. Most of the police actions are reported in the valley districts while crime in the hill districts is very likely not reported or assumed to be addressed through local customs. There are other issues as well mostly tied to governance, execution and implementation. But without going into details assuming the problems are already familiar since the violence is very much making headlines, I'll simply go to the next part.

Economic: The sate borrowings is almost 50% of the GDSP. The recommended debt to GDSP ratio is 20-25%. The almost 90%~ of expenditure in relation to receipts means the state of Manipur is not prepared for any eventuality. The Manipur violence 2023, floods and almost no rehabilitation and relief measures or disaster response is an example. The Negative opening balance of the state of Manipur means the state is already in the red. The state is simply unable to meet its own expenses. Negative gross fiscal deficit and negative surplus running on average negative of 1000-2000 crores indicates the state is already in a severe financial crisis.

Phased Approach Proposal

Each phase is 5 years long. All under the ambit of the state. For efficacy, each process can follow the 'Pareto Model' we use in Quality Assurance. This because we have limited means to address problems. The 80:20 rule. Given a 3 set of 5-year plan, we should be able to mitigate the crisis in 15 years. This assuming, without any failure in any process or function.

- Phase 1: Acknowledge political reality and economic status and list all possible problems and possible solutions. Groundwork for consensus building- reconciliation, ethnic, insurgence, governance, bureaucracy, economic and political. *De-radicalization measures*, absorbing the youth into Manipur Rifles (a joint sate-central upgrade) and *strengthening the Manipur Rifles. Inter-district road connections* to reduce ethnic tensions and improve security coverage. *Social reform measures and improved policing*. More emphasis on security & remedial measures in this step including the issue of IDPs.

- Phase 2: Restructuring, democratic solutions and process application and possibly, intake of all protest, denial, allegations etc. Greater autonomy demands, Social demands, representation issues, devolution/decentralization, and the much talked about erosion of federal structure in this step 2. More emphasis on political issues/restructuring in this step.

- Phase 3: Establish new townships if needed. *Integration efforts*, redefining the 'Manipuri Identity'. Inculcating these values in everyday life and education. If step 1 and 2 is successful, I'll assume the political climate will be conducive for business. More emphasis on economic measures in this step. Creation of *SEZ islands* in the hills and valley. Creation of new &

additional *economic corridors* (3 in total). Effectively curbing resource
- domination issues while allowing 'non-Manipuri' participants in a controlled environment.

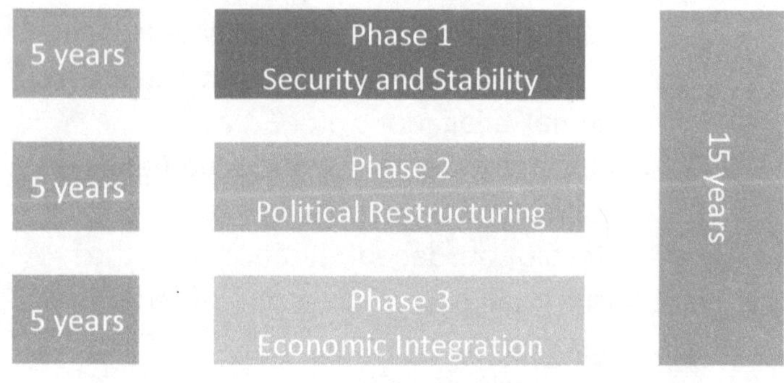

Fig. Visualization of the 15-year phased process/function.

In relation to the phased approach, since social and political dynamics will not follow a linear progression, the following options can be adopted in line with the critical approach as outlined in phases above.

Modular Approach

Assuming the government has the resources to take up multiple issues simultaneously. If the phased approach is too structured and we want to introduce a module-based approach for faster execution. Perhaps we can break down major heads into the following independent modules;

- Political: Governance in relation to greater autonomy, aligning with local specificities, resource distribution, reconciliation, ethnic issues, bureaucracy, representation issues.

- Security: The formation of Manipur Regiment or upgradation of Manipur Rifles into a joint state-center security force. Strengthening and increasing effectiveness of state police.

- Economic: The SEZ models, or creating protected economic corridors (PECs). For example, Moreh-Imphal-Jiribam. Infrastructure push, inter district road network development. Investments in capital

and infra projects. Establishing new
townships.

- Social: De radicalization measures, Integration efforts, redefining the 'Manipuri Identity'. Inculcating these values in everyday life and education. Social reform measures.

Hybrid Approach

If the above two approach is too rigid and the dynamics demand a more adaptable model. The decision makers can take the hybrid model. For example, the government can decide a phased security model while combining independent political, social and economic modules. A simultaneous approach including all models can put the states resources under severe stress.

Recursive Policies

Policing: Since the FIR data are now entered in the systems. It should be possible to establish data driven guided policies to monitor and mitigate three main enabling crimes – narcotics, arms and organized crime, increasing security presence actions where the data shows increased incidences. This can become part of an EWS (Early Warning System). The state can expand the recursive methodology to other areas with the pace of development and upgrade in its own mechanism; social and development.

In the sampling exercise the policing ratio from the available records indicated *extremely low policing records from the hill districts*. This needs to be corrected. There is no understanding if the life and property in the hills is even protected. The absence of executive in the hills appear to be a threat to state's integrity. Better policing can help mitigate ethnic divide and increase public confidence in the government.

Other things that may interest, the living quarters of the employees need to be upgraded to the standards expected. There has to be an established standard which needs to be adhered to in order to set a benchmark against which quality of life should be assessed regularly (recursive). This upkeep alone may help boost the morale of the armed forces and reduce posting and transfer avoidance.

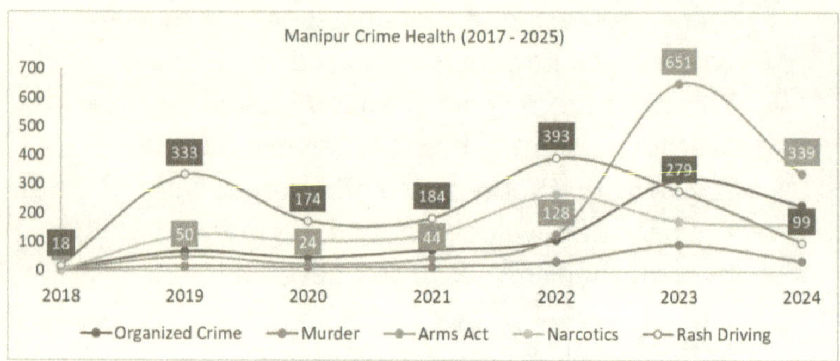

Manipur Crime Health (2017 - 2025)
700
600
500
400
300
200
100
0
2018
2019
2020
2021
2022
2023
2024
18
333
174
184
393
651
279
339
50
24
44
128
99
Organized Crime
Murder
Arms Act
Narcotics
Rash Driving

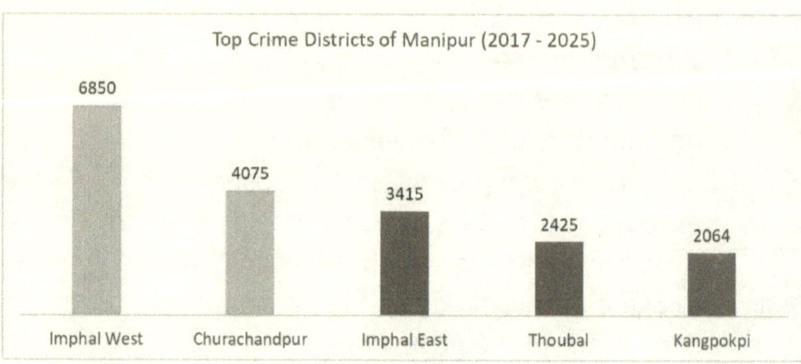

Top Crime Districts of Manipur (2017 - 2025)
6850
4075
3415
2425
2064
Imphal West
Churachandpur
Imphal East
Thoubal
Kangpokpi

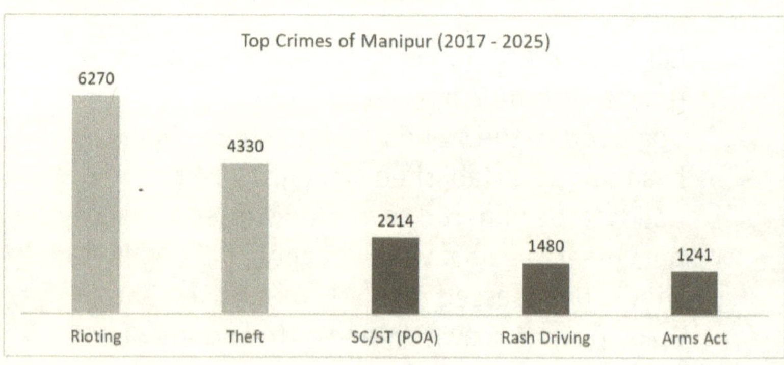

Top Crimes of Manipur (2017 - 2025)
6270
4330
2214
1480
1241
Rioting
Theft
SC/ST (POA)
Rash Driving
Arms Act

Figure: The figure on the right is a broad understanding of the crime trend in Manipur from all available records starting 2017 and also including the 2023 event. In relation to the communal violence that broke out the key districts involved as expected included the main population centers of the two communities. The line graph at the top includes data till 2025 to create and analyze trend. The main drivers of crime already being highlighted.

Nature of the data: The data was not readily useable and had to be categorized into categories based on *similar Acts or Laws*. *Organized crime* involves insurgency, mob, armed gangs and such, murders encompass all kinds of murders, arms act has been separately dealt with in the wake of the arms loot from police armories.

A more detailed date would have elicited better information but that will be too exhaustive so to keep it brief we have selected main crime enabling categories.

Second graph indicates nature of crime before the violence broke out in order to facilitate differentiation patterns for study.

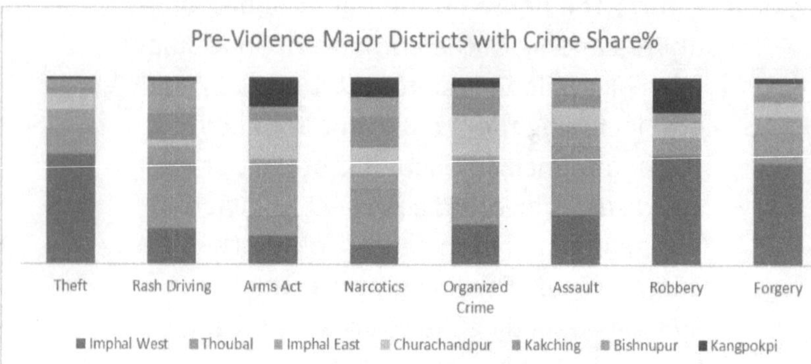

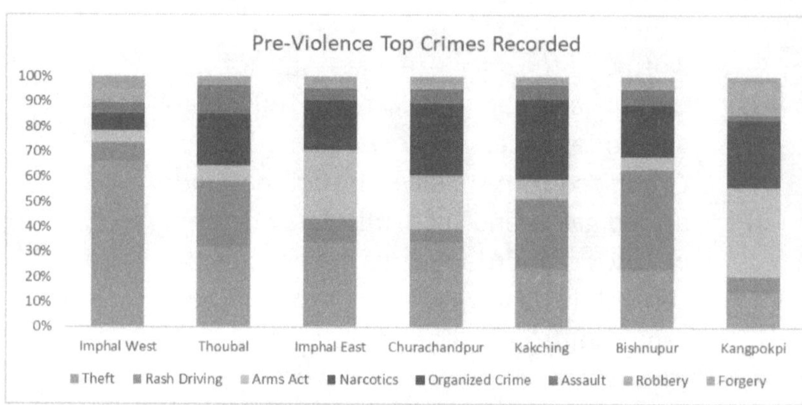

The data above is indicative of crimes in major population centers and the nature of the crime. Only 6 (six) select districts is taken here because the other districts did not have much data. The percentages however, in a tabular format;

District	Policing Share %
Imphal West	28.08%
Thoubal	27.09%
Kakching	11.36%
Bishnupur	8.60%
Imphal East	5.19%
Churachandpur	9.64%
Kangpokpi	3.41%
Tengnoupal	1.89%
Senapati	1.43%
Ukhrul	1.18%
Jiribam	0.61%
Kamjong	0.58%
Noney	0.53%
Chandel	0.29%
Tamenglong	0.12%

The calculations are based on number of FIRs recorded. Time period is from 2017 to

2025. The urban centers have sizeable police presence while the hill districts have almost negligible police presence. Tamenglong owing to its difficult terrain remains the most neglected district. In the span of 30 years, the district has witnessed extortions from salaried employees deducted straight from the bank, this incident is as recent as 2016. It has now given birth to a new faction, the ZUF (Zeliangrong United Front) and recent news indicate the faction will not work together with the larger organization under the NSCN umbrella.

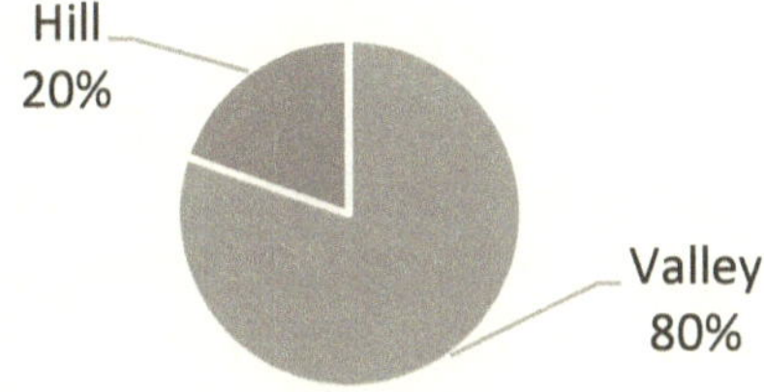

Policing Share Pre-Violence 2016 - 2022
Hill
20%
Valley
80%

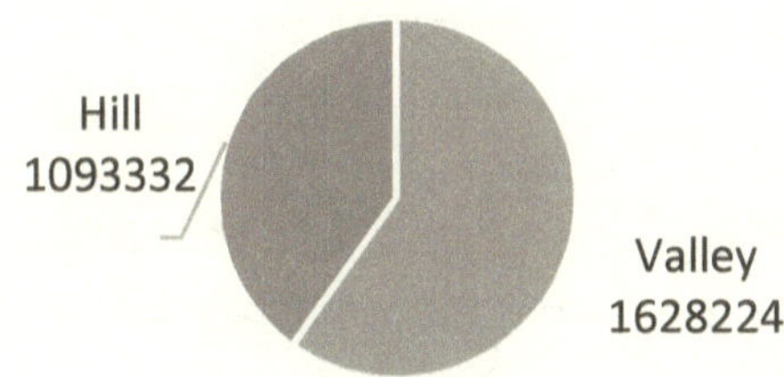

Popn No.s (2011 Census)
Hill
1093332
Valley
1628224

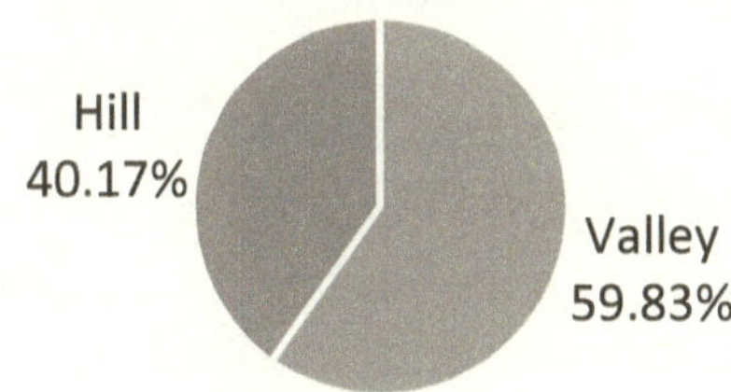

Popn % (2011 Census)
Hill
40.17%
Valley
59.83%

The ratios in the previous pages indicates the distribution categorized into hill and valley. While 40.17% of Manipur population resides in the hills the policing based on the data indicates just 20% coverage. Tribal customary judicial may play a role here, but in essence it simply translates into law-and-order problem. The customary laws as understood is not codified and follows a loose agreement which may not translate into justice.

Case 1: This is a case that happened within the Anal community. The case was against the wife on charges of adultery. The case was brought to the village authorities with the aim to divorce the wife. The wife was shamed and chased out from the house and she came to her maternal home on foot crossing the rivers and fields. The moment I saw her she cried and cried and told the family what took place.

'If only he wanted to divorce me, why didn't he say so. Why give me a bad name and allege crimes I have not committed all I did was take care of the family and worked the fields. Father, father look what they did to me.'

So, summarily she couldn't win the case, the case went in favor of the husband and the divorce came. And according to the customs, the family had to tender a formal apology and sacrifice an animal, which apparently is a high price according to the customs.

Case 2: The widow comes home to her father owing to the fact that her husband's family decided to have absolutely no relations with her or her children. This is a fairly recent case. And since the father was a Meitei, the village authority decided not to allow them to settle in the village. The widow lost the case, but her brother afforded her a small part of his plot since they have nowhere else to go. In contrast another widow who also married a Meitei was given a plot of land by the village authorities.

In both the case we see there is an element of convenience and there is no justice as such that the authorities claim under the Village Authority Act. Of course, there are matters that relate to the state's administration but summarily it fuels unrest, hate, partisanship and communalism within the society itself. There is a clear division of *'us' and 'them', which is perpetuated by the system itself*

Crime Spatial Overview

Five select districts is used here on Pareto Principle, further classifying the type of crimes that that need to be addressed at the earliest specified in the second graph.
The additional graphs allow the authorities to focus police actions where it is required in order to enforce law and order at the earliest.

The map here is indicative of pre and post 2023 violence and gives a broad spatial overview and understanding of the crime pattern or law and order. Pre 2023 distribution of crimes recorded in major population centers. The hill districts record almost no crime.

Post 2023 distribution of crimes recorded in major population centers. The hill districts still record almost no crime. But major centers where kuki community reside records a sharp increase of crime rate.

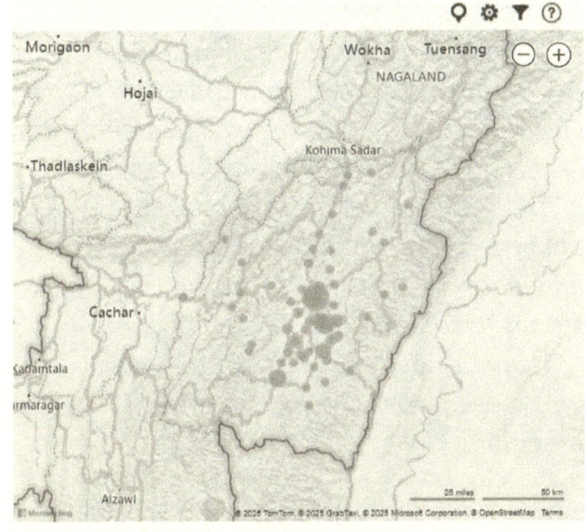

Morigaon
Wokha
Tuensang
NAGALAND
Hojai
Kohima Sadar
Thadlaskein
Cachar
Kadamtala
irmaragar
Aizawl
25 miles
50 km
© 2025 TomTom, © 2025 GrabTaxi, © 2025 Microsoft Corporation, © OpenStreetMap   Terms

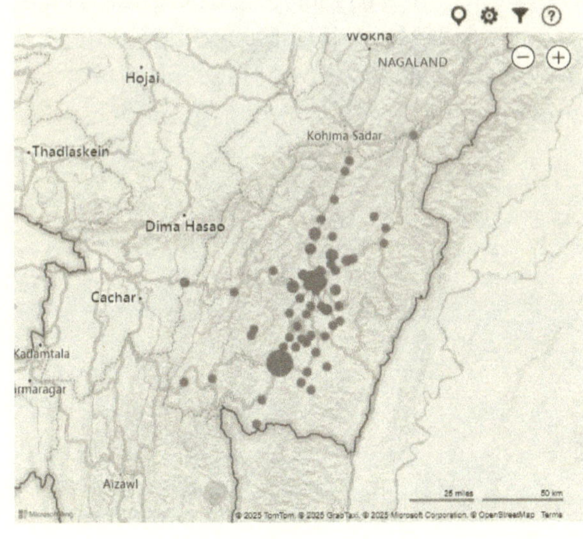

Wokha
NAGALAND
Hojai
Kohima Sadar
Thadlaskein
Dima Hasao
Cachar
Kadamtala
irmaragar
Aizawl
25 miles
50 km
© 2025 TomTom, © 2025 GrabTaxi, © 2025 Microsoft Corporation, © OpenStreetMap   Terms

Further breakdown of crime pattern in relation to three most pressing crimes – Arms, Narcotics and Organized Crime (Triplets). The 'Triplets' is used to identify its occurrence and frequency in the major districts, Churachandpur, Imphal East, Thoubal are the main focus areas to eliminate the 'Triplets.' Arresting the 'Triplet' stands to solve a huge portion of crime in Manipur. Under each district, the main localities of occurrence is identified for better precision.

The diagrams below provide a broader understanding of crime patterns and prevalence, this to facilitate police forces to act on crimes that, if not acted upon may be understood as absence of law and order – in short public perception management.

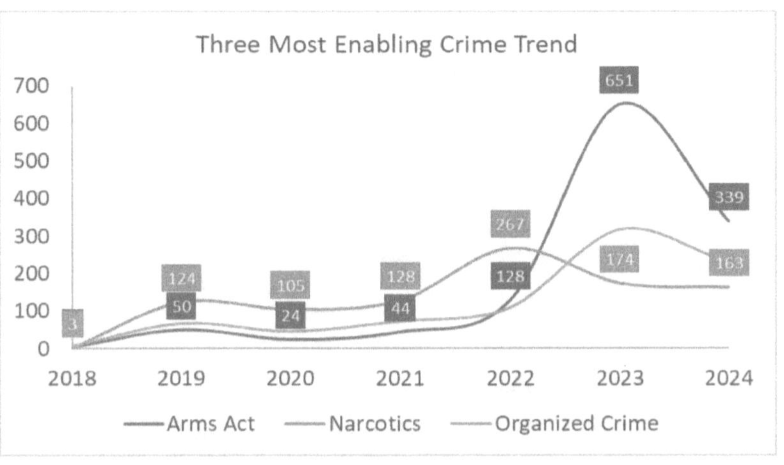

The figures indicate district wise crime rate taking the 'triplets' as the major concern. The assumption being the control of the distribution and prevention of incidences can drastically reduce all other crimes. Without the enablers the other crimes will have a 'ripple effect.' The focus is again on 4 main districts and 4 major localities in each district following the *pareto principle*.
The sampling size is from 2018-2024.
Narcotic crimes is highest in the following centers; *Kakching, Thoubal. Lilong. Churachandpur*

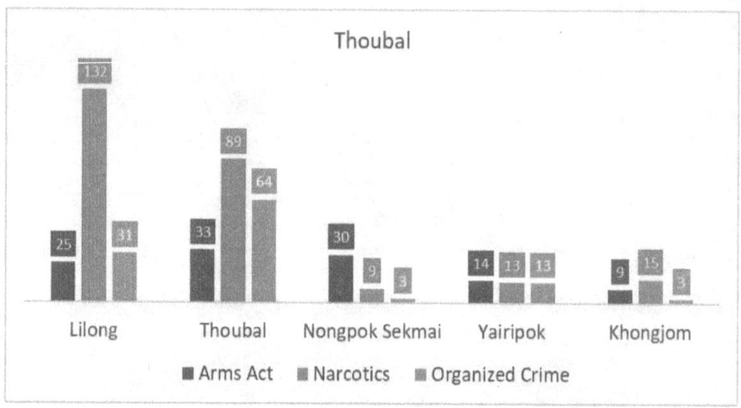

Thoubal
132
89
64
25
33
31
30
9
3
14
13
13
9
15
3
Lilong
Thoubal
Nongpok Sekmai
Yairipok
Khongjom
Arms Act
Narcotics
Organized Crime

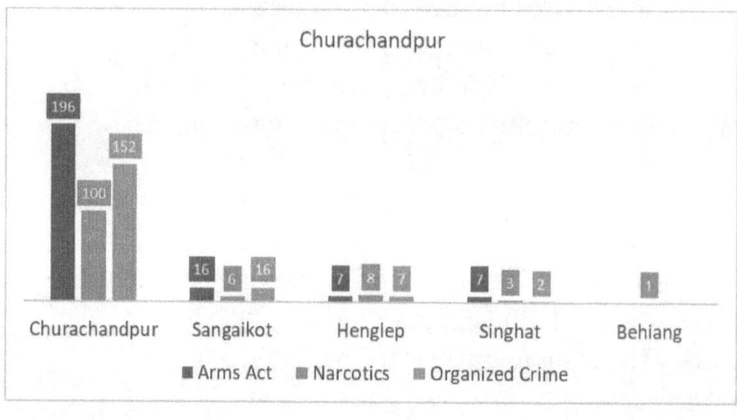

Churachandpur
196
100
152
16
6
16
7
8
7
7
3
2
1
Churachandpur
Sangaikot
Henglep
Singhat
Behiang
Arms Act
Narcotics
Organized Crime

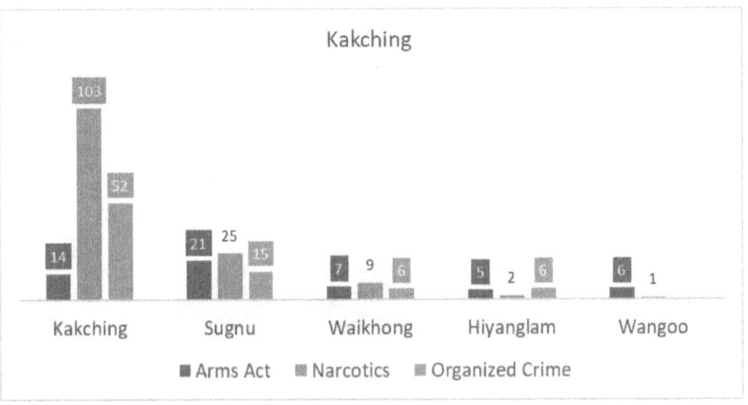

Kakching
103
52
14
21
25
15
7
9
6
5
2
6
6
1
Kakching
Sugnu
Waikhong
Hiyanglam
Wangoo
Arms Act
Narcotics
Organized Crime

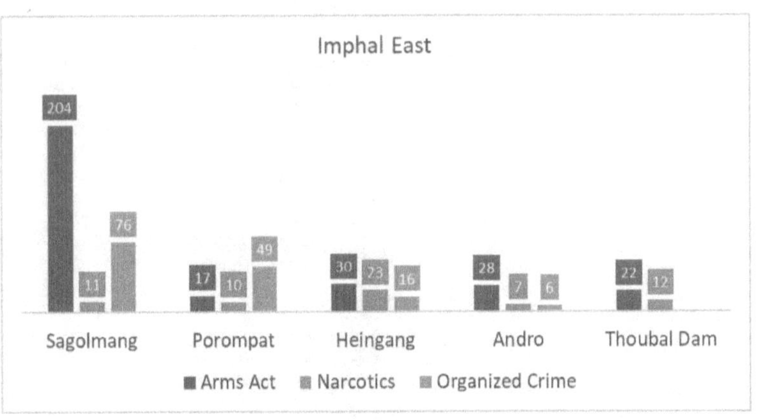

Imphal East
204
76
11
17
10
49
30
23
16
28
7
6
22
12
Sagolmang
Porompat
Heingang
Andro
Thoubal Dam
Arms Act
Narcotics
Organized Crime

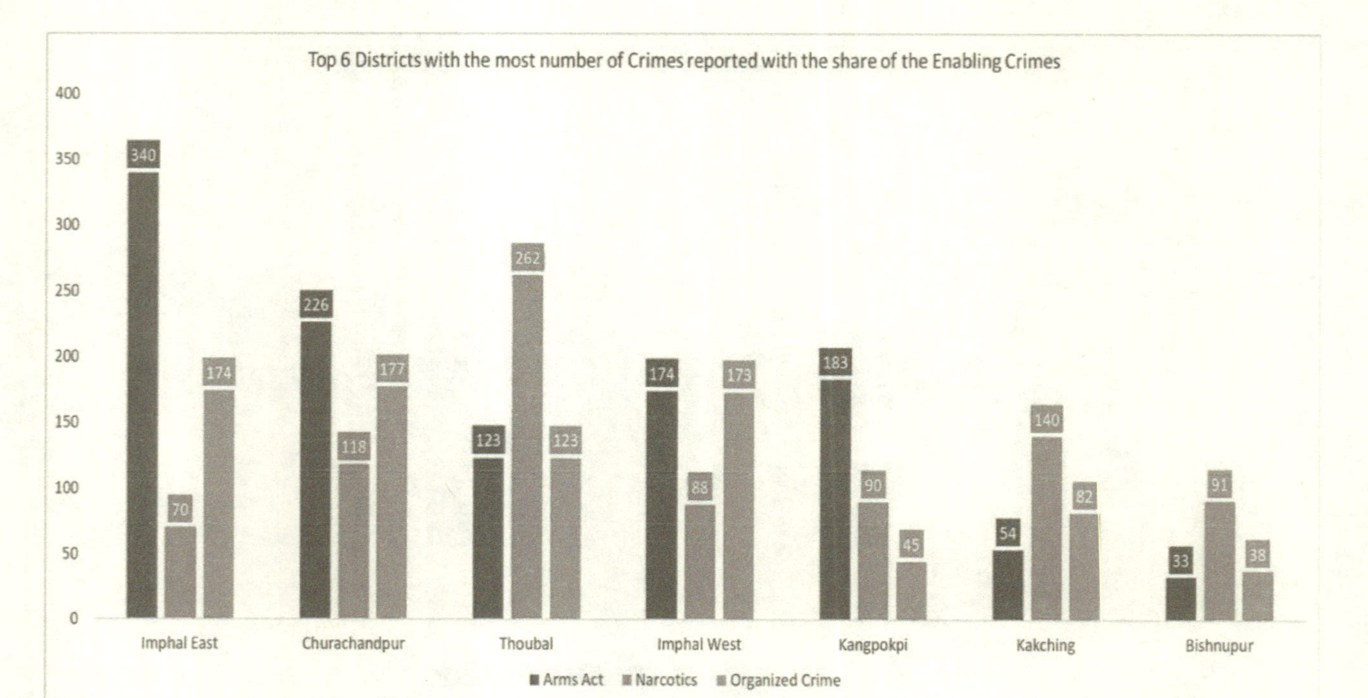

Top 6 Districts with the most number of Crimes reported with the share of the Enabling Crimes
400
350
300
250
200
150
100
50
0
Imphal East
Churachandpur
Thoubal
Imphal West
Kangpokpi
Kakching
Bishnupur
340
70
174
226
118
177
123
262
123
174
88
173
183
90
45
54
140
82
33
91
38
Arms Act
Narcotics
Organized Crime

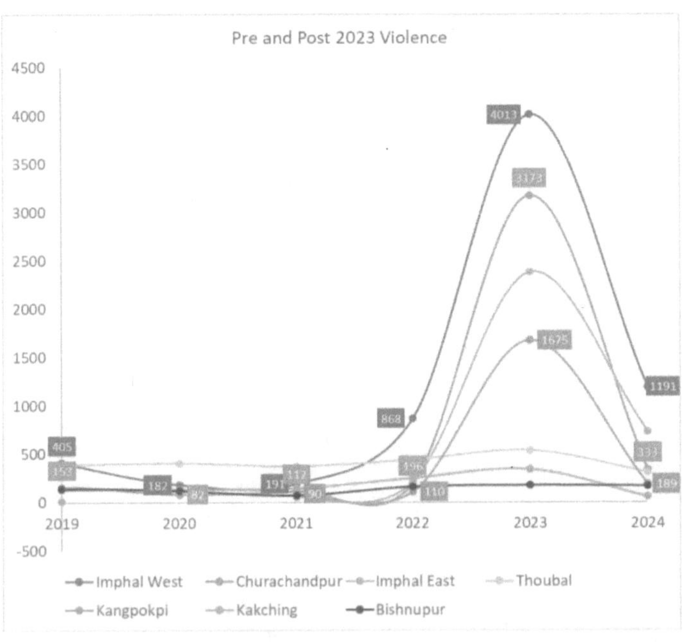

Pre and Post 2023 Violence
4500
4000
3500
3000
2500
2000
1500
1000
500
0
-500
2019
2020
2021
2022
2023
2024
405
353
182
82
191
112
90
496
110
868
4013
3373
1675
1191
333
189
Imphal West
Churachandpur
Imphal East
Thoubal
Kangpokpi
Kakching
Bishnupur

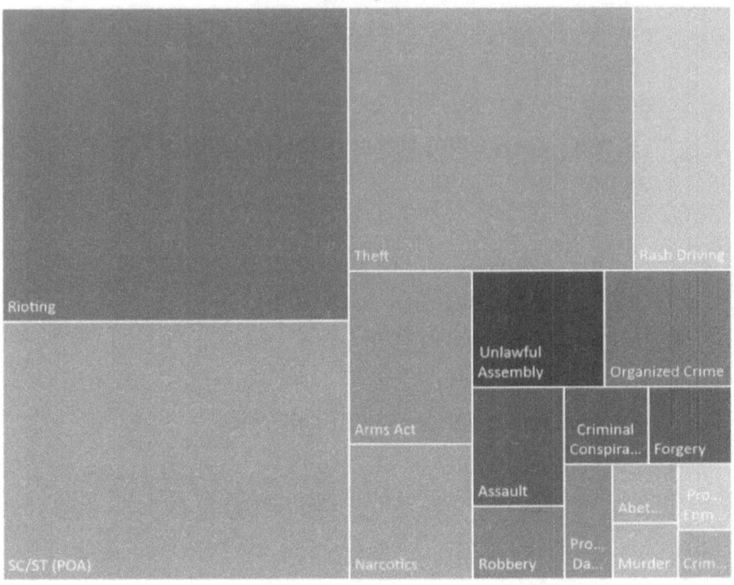

Crime Share (Average of 2017-2025)
Rioting
SC/ST (POA)
Theft
Arms Act
Narcotics
Unlawful Assembly
Assault
Robbery
Rash Driving
Organized Crime
Criminal Conspira...
Forgery
Abet...
Pro... Da...
Murder
Pro... Enm...
Crim...

The diagrams above are indicative of crimes, the numbers indicate the number of FIRs recorded in each year in the 7 districts as shown.

The figure below the trend indicates the size of crimes recorded so far. It is cumulative, hence rioting and SC/ST POA FIRs have far exceeded other 'traditional' crimes.

Incremental Model

Given the government changes every 5 years, if the continuity is in question. The government can adopt an incremental model for select programs, where target areas can be divided into major population centers with completion rates as basis. For example;

- Immediate compensatory and or rehabilitation measures.
- Case resolution in relation to reconciliations.
- Skill and Upskill programs.
- Job placement and or accommodation assistance if any.

Start- Suspend- Stop Model

If in the course of formulating new and experimental policies or expensive/sensitive or/labor intensive policies, whichever the case is. The authorities can follow a dialectical method to promulgate new policies and adopt a start-suspend-stop model to test effectiveness and or feedback and redeploy. For example, testing possible solutions agreed upon in phase 1, it will save the government from instability and possible major social backlash.

The entire phased model can follow this model. This can also be applied to modular or incremental models. This can also be used to apply Acts already in force but not enforced.

The benefits of this model;

- Risk management, evaluation and assessment opportunity
- Example as such integration/replication models
- Room for tactical decision making etc.

Case 1: Phased application of The Manipur Hill Areas (Acquisition of Chiefs' Rights) Act, 1967. Assuming this is done in a phased manner for example smaller villages or an area and suspend the operation. And revive the operation in another village and suspend after inducting the previous villages into a ADC (Autonomous District Council) model.

Conclusion

The summary attempts to include the 'nature of the society', to model and re-align 'governance 'with the community's specificities. It could be applied in all three levels to address issues concerning administration; political (local) and economic. The state being unable to service itself without higher than recommended borrowing shares, it must direct expenses in capital and infrastructure projects – roads, water, electricity. While the phased approach is most cost effective it assumes predictable outcomes. The other two approaches are more dynamic but it will put considerable strain on resources. While the outcomes become more unpredictable. The phased model in comparison will be more manageable and will put less strain on resources.

The paper, are all but 'broad attempts' since the definition of these processes and functions cannot come from the paper alone. It recognizes   that processes cannot always follow a sequential step that way. The success of this model needs participation from all sections. The government, public, institutions, the civil societies and the various organizations. It only attempts to breakdown the issues into recognizable component parts that should be manageable and put into processes that can be measured and monitored. The project is ambitious as it envisages solution within a 15 fifteen-year timeline. The efficiency of which can only be ascertained at completion. This follows the previous paper, that recognizes the political reality of the tribals and Manipuri in general. In effect to the papers the published article, *'Manipur needs to affirm her tribal roots (Sangai Express, also included in the previous chapter)',* need to be accounted in order to set the political environment for the recovery process and to avoid the fate of Tripura while not entirely closing the state like that of North Korea. It also gives each successive government a clear goal to attain in each term. The specificities and mechanisms of each phase will be the government's prerogative.

The National Register of Citizens

Following the 2003, Citizenship Amendment Act, the NRC was created to maintain a register of all Indian citizens. This was followed by the Citizenship Amendment Act, 2019 to accelerate the naturalization process of persecuted Hindus, Christians, Parsis, Jain religious minority communities of Pakistan, Bangladesh and Afghanistan.

NRC: Why 1961 as base year for Manipur and not 1951.

The debate on the base year in summary;

1951: Manipur risk expelling too many and creating hostile political forces that will never rest. It risks creating too many stateless "people".

1961: It gives some room and also provides legally actionable segregation based on concrete evidence of state formation and its history.

Although it's theoretical, 1961 is the middle path. This coincides with Assam protest and this proposal is well grounded in political events surrounding Manipur of that time. For those arguing for 1951, perhaps they need to reason and go through not just the "census" but political developments around 1951 & 1961.

We need to reference the history and avoid political rhetorics. While the argument of 1961, here presents opposing opinions it does not invalidate the argument of 1951 wholly, a debate on the stand why 1951 is just and logical should also be considered and properly investigated. The opinion however, 1951 census record is unreliable too, the census likely excludes citizens in the hinterlands. Authorities can supplement on this argument. It risks alienating Manipuris themselves owing to unreliable method of "sampling" or data collection of that time, which is undeniably less reliable than 1961. The previous "ex-CM" of Manipur's decision in suggesting 1961 as the base year is not just right in making this decision but it is pragmatic and politically "correct." It is a well-balanced approach considering the future stability of Manipur State.

For Manipur, this is not a compromise, rather its a strategic decision. If at all possible it should extend to 1971, a year before its state formation. The precedent being Assam NRC 1971. The decision made should aim at long term- "Stability". The very idea of why NRC is necessary anyway.

1951- Less reliable data
1961- Strategic & pragmatic
1971- More reliable data

In relation to the apprehension from the hill districts, on the other hand the Meiteis do not have the economic power to purchase dominate 90% of Manipur state. The exorbitant rates the Meiteis will pay to the tribals for the plot of land in relation to the economics of demand and supply only stand to make create *'neo-rich'* tribals. It will create wealthy tribals. It simply follows the norm of the;

"Creation of wealth".

The apprehensions therefore, seems to emanate from a political aspiration "only" rather than an honest grievance of the common tribal folk. Anthropologically, Meiteis are anyway tribal. There are many Meiteis who have tribal relatives now as well. I'm of that generation who have a mix parentage. It is imperative to separate administration from identity, otherwise we risk tribal feuds.

Conclusion

The theories are based on the assumption that ideologies cannot be suppressed, the correct way of handling growing ideologies is by providing guidance so that they do not develop into social problems that will ultimately culminate in events like the May 3rd event in Manipur. The paper attempts to be more objective and solution oriented by presenting problems that are otherwise left to speculations and divided school of thought. The *Three State Theory* in essence recognizes the political reality in that sense and formulates a policy that separates administration from identity. It is in other words akin to district organization but with slightly different administration that aligns with local specificities. That way it makes governance more relevant and creates a solid administrative structure that binds the three objects together under the 'State.' The use of empirical data to analyze law and order situation is a start for policing that can help address major problems that pose a challenge to the society. It is hoped that such analysis can provide the police with the knowledge of what to do and where to act with precision and effect. The demand for Scheduled Tribes status for the Meiteis takes precedence from Bodoland Territorial Council.

In relation to the National Register of Citizens which is currently in the news, perhaps the government can start with the base year 1961, and three months later or 6 months later cite data consistency issues and move to the more appropriate 1971 as the base year.

The treatise or theories here are meant to provoke thought and are not final solutions as they may appear. It will be more prudent to present critical or counter arguments on the ideas made so far and perhaps include it further discussions to bring about a more comprehensive and practical solution to problems. The ideas should not become the 'de facto' foundation of other ideologies or become reason for justifying actions.

Redlands

Since the Redlands,
Umpteenth times,
The skies wept.

Since the Redlands,
Countless names,
The rivers swallowed.

Since the Redlands,
Seldom marched,
Often, two steps back.

Since the Redlands,
Random hopes,
Cherished dreams.

***